M000076653

Success With
Writing

SCHOLASTIC

Scholastic Inc. grants teachers permission to photocopy the reproducible pages from this book for classroom use. No other part of this publication may be reproduced in whole or in part, or stored in a retrieval system, or transmitted in any form or by any means, electronic, mechanical, photocopying, recording, or otherwise without written permission of the publisher. For information regarding permission, write to Scholastic Inc., 557 Broadway, New York, NY 10012.

Editor: Ourania Papacharalambous
Cover design by Tannaz Fassihi; cover illustration by Kevin Zimmer
Interior design by Cynthia Ng
Interior illustrations by Maarten Lenoir (6, 8–9, 11, 13–14, 17, 23, 32, 36–37, 40, 42); Doug Jones (spot art)
All other images © Shutterstock.com

ISBN 978-1-338-79872-2
Scholastic Inc., 557 Broadway, New York, NY 10012
Copyright © 2022 Scholastic Inc.
All rights reserved. Printed in the U.S.A.
First printing, January 2022
1 2 3 4 5 6 7 8 9 10   40 29 28 27 26 25 24 23 22

INTRODUCTION

One of the greatest challenges teachers and parents face is helping children develop independent writing skills. Each writing experience is unique and individualized. The high-interest topics and engaging exercises in *Scholastic Success With Writing* will both stimulate and encourage children as they develop their writing skills. On page 4, you will find a list of the key skills covered in the activities throughout this book. These grade-appropriate skills can be used in daily writing assignments such as journals, stories, and letters to help build confident, independent writers. Like a stepladder, this book will help children reach the next level of independent writing.

TABLE OF CONTENTS

Grade-Appropriate Skills Covered in *Scholastic Success With Writing: Grade 2*

Know and use various text features to locate key facts or information in a text efficiently.

Know and apply grade-level phonics and word analysis skills in decoding words.

Recognize and read grade-appropriate irregularly spelled words.

Write narratives that recount a well-elaborated event or short sequence of events, include details to describe actions, thoughts, and feelings, use temporal words to signal event order, and provide a sense of closure.

Demonstrate command of the conventions of standard English grammar and usage when writing or speaking.

Use collective nouns.

Form and use frequently occurring irregular plural nouns.

Form and use the past tense of frequently occurring irregular verbs.

Use adjectives and adverbs, and choose between them depending on what is to be modified.

Produce, expand, and rearrange complete simple and compound sentences.

Demonstrate command of the conventions of standard English capitalization, punctuation, and spelling when writing.

Use commas in greetings and closings of letters.

Generalize learned spelling patterns when writing words.

Use knowledge of language and its conventions when writing, speaking, reading, or listening.

Demonstrate understanding of word relationships and nuances in word meanings.

Distinguish shades of meaning among closely related verbs and closely related adjectives.

Use words and phrases acquired through conversations, reading and being read to, and responding to texts, including using adjectives and adverbs to describe.

© Scholastic Inc.

You're Sharp!

Circle the words that show the correct way
to begin each sentence.

A sentence
begins with a
capital letter.

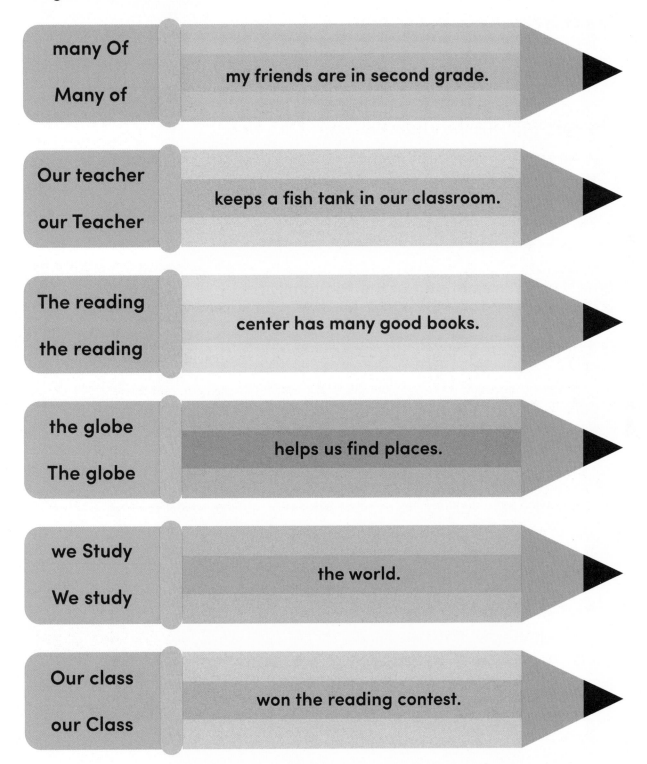

many Of

Many of

my friends are in second grade.

Our teacher

our Teacher

keeps a fish tank in our classroom.

The reading

the reading

center has many good books.

the globe

The globe

helps us find places.

we Study

We study

the world.

Our class

our Class

won the reading contest.

© Scholastic Inc.

A Whale of a Sentence

Rewrite the sentences using capital letters and periods.

A **telling sentence** begins with a **capital letter** and ends with a **period.**

1 the blue whale has no teeth

_____

2 the blue whale is the largest animal in the world

_____

_____

3 blue whales are not part of the fish family

_____

_____

4 blue whales eat tiny shrimp-like sea creatures

_____

_____

5 blue whales have two blowholes

_____

_____

© Scholastic Inc.

That Sounds Fishy to Me

Write a sentence about each fish. Remember to tell a complete idea.

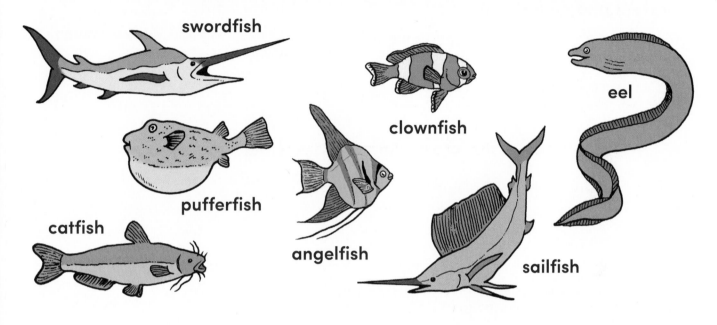

swordfish

clownfish

eel

pufferfish

angelfish

catfish

sailfish

1 <u>The swordfish has a long snout.</u>

2 _____

3 _____

4 _____

5 _____

6 _____

7 _____

© Scholastic Inc.

Ask Mother Goose

Rewrite the questions using capital letters and question marks.

A sentence that asks a question ends with a **question mark (?)**.

It often begins with one of these words:

Who	*What*	*Where*	*When*
Why	*Will*	*Could*	*How*

1 where is the king's castle

_____

2 who helped Humpty Dumpty

_____

3 why did the cow jump over the moon

_____

4 will the frog become a prince

_____

5 could the three mice see

_____

© Scholastic Inc.

Ask the Wolf

Imagine that you could meet the Big Bad Wolf. What questions would you ask him about Little Red Riding Hood and the Three Little Pigs? Use a different beginning word for each question you write.

An **asking sentence** begins with a **capital letter** and ends with a **question mark (?)**. It often begins with one of these words:

How	Can	Would
Did	Is	Should

1. How _____

2. Did _____

3. Can _____

1. Is _____

2. Should _____

3. Would _____

Sunny Sentences

**Rewrite each
sentence correctly.**

Every sentence begins
with a **capital letter**.

A **telling sentence** ends
with a **period (.)**.

An **asking sentence** ends
with a **question mark (?)**.

1 the sun is the closest star to Earth

_____

2 the sun is not the brightest star

_____

3 what is the temperature of the sun

_____

4 the sun is a ball of hot gas

_____

5 how large is the sun

_____

6 it takes about eight minutes for the sun's light to reach Earth

_____

© Scholastic Inc.

Camp Fiddlestick

Write three statements and three questions about the picture.

A telling sentence is called a **statement**. An asking sentence is called a **question**. Now ask yourself:

How do sentences begin?
How do statements end?
How do questions end?

Statements:

1 _____

2 _____

3 _____

Questions:

1 _____

2 _____

3 _____

A Happy Camper

Complete each sentence below.

1. Every sentence begins with a _____.

2. A statement ends with a _____.

3. A question ends with a _____.

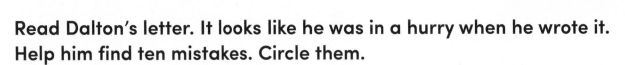

Read Dalton's letter. It looks like he was in a hurry when he wrote it. Help him find ten mistakes. Circle them.

> Dear Mom and Dad,
>
>   camp is so cool? today we went swimming? do you know what I like best about camp. fishing is my favorite thing to do. did you feed my hamster. I really miss you?
>
>   Love,
>   Dalton

Choose two questions and two statements from Dalton's letter. Rewrite each correctly.

1. _____

2. _____

3. _____

4. _____

© Scholastic Inc.

A Day at the Beach

Finish each sentence by putting a period, a question mark, or an exclamation point in the shell at the end.

A sentence that shows strong feeling or excitement is called an **exclamation**. It ends with an **exclamation point (!)**. For example: *Look at that shark!*

1. Jamie will be at the beach today

2. Did you bring the beach ball

3. Look at the size of the waves

4. Where did I leave my sunglasses

5. Mom put snacks in the beach bag

6. Watch out for that jellyfish

7. Do you want to build a sandcastle

8. The sun is bright today

9. Did you see that sailboat

10. Don't step on that starfish

11. It is windy near the seashore

12. Should we put up an umbrella

© Scholastic Inc.

Seashore Sentences

Write a statement (S), a question (Q), and an exclamation (E) about each picture.

S _____

_____

Q _____

_____

E _____

_____

S _____

_____

Q _____

_____

E _____

_____

© Scholastic Inc.

Building Blocks

A good sentence has a part that tells who or what the sentence is about. This is called the **subject**.

A good sentence has a part that tells what happens. This is called the **action**, or **verb**.

Make a list of possible subjects to complete each sentence.

_____ jumped the fence.

1 _____

2 _____

3 _____

_____ is too full.

1 _____

2 _____

3 _____

Make a list of possible actions to complete each sentence.

We _____ on the playground.

1 _____

2 _____

3 _____

The cowboy _____ on his horse.

1 _____

2 _____

3 _____

© Scholastic Inc.

Keep Building!

For each sentence, make a list of possible endings that tell where or when the action happens.

Some sentences have a part that tells where or when the action is happening.

The wind blew _____.

1 _____

2 _____

3 _____

The boy tripped _____.

1 _____

2 _____

3 _____

Complete each sentence.

1 _____ made us laugh last night.

2 The door leads _____.

3 The crowd _____ at the fair.

4 The paint bucket spilled _____.

5 _____ was never seen again.

6 The firefighter _____ into the fire truck.

© Scholastic Inc.

Get Your Ticket!

Write a sentence to match each picture. Be sure to include a subject, an action, and a part that tells where or when.

 ① <u>A boy climbs a tree in his backyard.</u>

② _____

 ③ _____

Slide Show

Write three sentences and
draw pictures to match.

A sentence is more interesting
when it includes a subject, an
action, and a part that tells
where or when.

subject	action	where or when

1 _____

subject	action	where or when

2 _____

subject	action	where or when

3 _____

© Scholastic Inc.

Country Roads

Add a describing word from the list to finish each sentence.

A good sentence uses describing words to help the reader "paint a picture" in his or her mind.

1. The _____ chicken laid _____ eggs in her nest.

2. The _____ barn keeps the animals _____ at night.

3. _____ carrots grow in the _____ garden.

4. Two _____ pigs sleep in the _____ pen.

5. The _____ cows drink from the _____ pond.

6. A _____ scarecrow frightens the _____ birds.

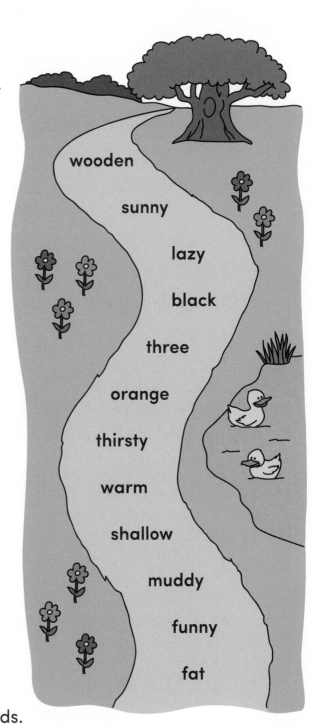

wooden

sunny

lazy

black

three

orange

thirsty

warm

shallow

muddy

funny

fat

© Scholastic Inc.

What Does It Feel Like?

Choose the best describing word to complete the sentence.

Describing words often provide information about something that we can discover with our senses.

1 Cotton candy is _____.

2 Before it is cooked, a potato is _____.

3 A peach's skin is _____.

4 A needle is _____.

5 Mashed potatoes are _____.

Word Bank

sharp

soft

fluffy

fuzzy

hard

Look at the words in the Word Bank.
Find and circle each word in the word search.

S	C	R	O	U	G	H	G	T	H
H	S	Y	K	V	A	D	M	H	E
I	Q	B	U	M	P	Y	X	I	L
N	S	M	O	O	T	H	O	C	H
Y	U	T	R	S	T	I	C	K	Y

Word Bank

thick

bumpy

rough

sticky

smooth

shiny

© Scholastic Inc.

Mystery Bags

Make a list of words that describe the object on each bag.

Describing words
help you imagine
how something
looks, feels, smells,
sounds, or tastes.

 Use a paper sack to make a real mystery bag. Place an object in the bag and give describing clues to someone at home. Can he or she guess the mystery object?

It's in the Bag

Add a describing word to each sentence.

1. My friend's _____ dog has fleas!

2. The _____ popcorn is in the big bowl.

3. How did the _____ worm get on the sidewalk?

4. The _____ ocean waves crashed against the rocks.

5. The _____ ball broke a window at school!

6. My _____ skin itched from poison ivy.

7. The two _____ squirrels chased each other up the tree.

8. The _____ sand felt good on my feet.

9. Are the _____ apples ready to be picked?

10. The _____ ball was hard to catch.

11. Is the _____ salamander hiding under the rock?

12. The _____ snow cone quickly melted.

© Scholastic Inc.

City Streets

Write a statement (S), a question (Q), and an exclamation (E) about the picture. Use each of the following describing words:

| fast | busy | crowded |

S _____

_____

Q _____

_____

E _____

_____

 Use describing words to write a sentence about your street.
Read the sentence to a friend.

Football Frenzy

Replace each  word to make the sentence more exact.

> A sentence is more interesting when it gives exact information.

1 The ball game starts soon .

The _____soccer_____ game starts _____now_____ .

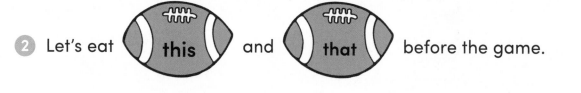

2 Let's eat this and that before the game.

Let's eat _____ and _____ before the game.

3 I hope they score some points.

I hope _____ score _____ points.

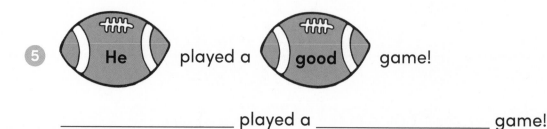

4 They were also there .

_____ were also _____ .

5 He played a good game!

_____ played a _____ game!

© Scholastic Inc.

Take Me Out to the Ball Game

Finish each sentence so that it answers the  question.

1. The players get to the stadium  **when**

_____

2. The team is excited because **why**

_____

3. The fans arrive in **what**

_____

4. Flags are flying **where**

_____

5. A man sings the "Star-Spangled Banner" **when**

_____

6. The fans cheer for **whom**

_____

7. The ball is hit **where**

_____

Cake and Ice Cream

Rewrite the sentences by combining their endings.

Two sentences that share the same subject can be combined to make one sentence by using the word *and*.

1 The party was fun.
The party was exciting.

<u>The party was fun and exciting.</u>

2 We blew up orange balloons.
We blew up green balloons.

_____

3 We ate cake.
We ate ice cream.

_____

4 The cake frosting was blue.
The cake frosting was yellow.

_____

5 We made a bookmark.
We made a clay pot.

_____

6 We brought games.
We brought presents.

_____

© Scholastic Inc.

Lunch Time!

Rewrite the sentences by combining their subjects.

Two sentences that share the same ending can also be combined to make one sentence.

① These peanuts are salty! These pretzels are salty!

These peanuts and pretzels are salty!

② The first graders eat lunch at noon. The second graders eat lunch at noon.

_____

_____

③ The napkins are on the table. The forks are on the table.

_____

_____

④ Are the muffins in the oven? Are the cookies in the oven?

_____

_____

⑤ Michael brought lunch today. Stephen brought lunch today.

_____

_____

© Scholastic Inc.

Great Gardening Tips

Combine the two sentences using the key word. Write a new sentence.

Sentences can also be combined to make them more interesting. Key words can help put two sentences together.

I will plan my garden. I am waiting for spring.

I will plan my garden while I am waiting for spring.

1 Fill a cup with water. Add some flower seeds.

_____

2 This will soften the seeds. They are hard.

_____

3 Fill another cup with dirt. The seeds soak in water.

_____

4 Bury the seeds in the cup. The dirt covers them.

_____

5 Add water to the plant. Do not add too much.

_____

6 Set the cup in the sun. The plant will grow.

_____

© Scholastic Inc.

Growing Sentences

**Write a combined sentence of your own.
Use the given key word to help you.**

1 while I watch TV while my mom
           makes lunch.

2 until _____

_____

3 because _____

_____

4 but _____

_____

5 or _____

_____

6 and _____

_____

© Scholastic Inc.

The Sky's the Limit

Fill in the blanks to make a list in each sentence.

Some sentences include a list. A **comma (,)** is used to separate each item in the list.

1. The birds built their nests using

   _____, _____,

   and _____.

2. I ate _____, _____,

   and _____ for breakfast.

3. We stayed with Grandma on _____,

   _____, and _____ nights.

4. I found _____, _____,

   and _____ in my party bag.

5. We played _____, _____,

   and _____ at summer camp.

6. The _____, _____,

   and _____ ate the corn we scattered.

© Scholastic Inc.

Up, Up, and Away

Write a sentence that includes a list of the words that are given.

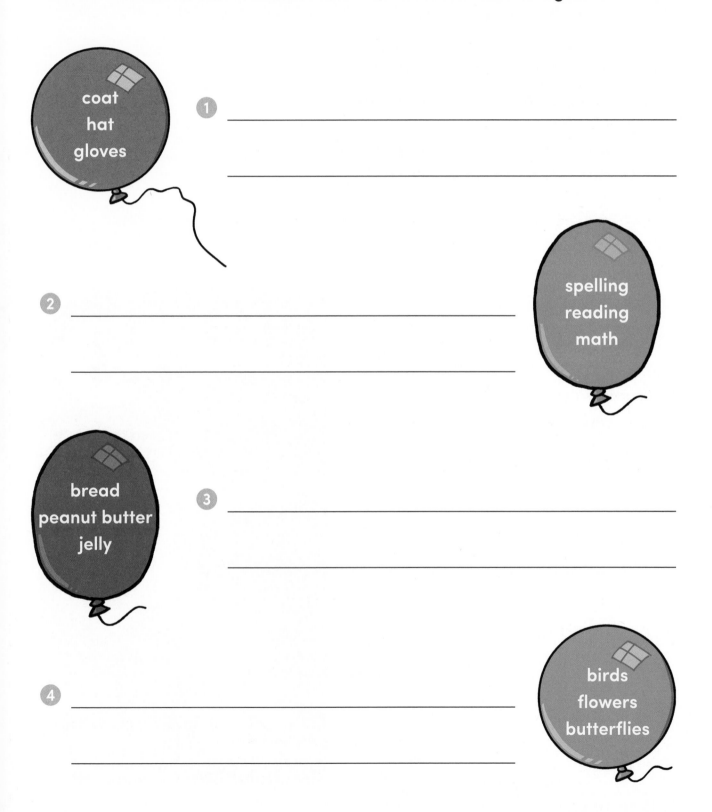

coat
hat
gloves

1 _____

_____

2 _____

_____

spelling
reading
math

bread
peanut butter
jelly

3 _____

_____

4 _____

_____

birds
flowers
butterflies

Out of This World

Use the proofreading marks to correct the two mistakes in each sentence.

> After you write a sentence, go back and look for mistakes. This is called **proofreading** your work.

m̲a̲r̲s̲ = Make a capital letter.	? = Add a question mark.	! = Add an exclamation point.
· = Add a period.	, = Add a comma.	☐ = Add a word. (Write a describing word in the box.)

1. Sometimes I can see mars Jupiter, and Saturn with my telescope.

☐

2. There are ∧ stars in our galaxy

☐

3. comets are ∧ pieces of ice and rock.

☐

4. The sun is really a ∧ star

5. is there life on any other planet

☐

6. Look at that ∧ shooting star

7. can you imagine traveling in space

© Scholastic Inc.

Smart About Saturn

Matthew's science report has nine mistakes. Use proofreading marks to correct his work. Then rewrite the report. Add at least two describing words to the report.

Saturn
by Matthew

Saturn is famous for the rings that surround it? its rings are made of ice, rock and dirt. The rings circle around the planet! Saturn is made mostly of gas? saturn's gases are lighter than water That means Saturn would float if you put it into a tub of water Saturn has more than 60 moons

_____

_____

_____

_____

Banana-Rama

Color the word that is missing from each sentence.

1. We _____ a spelling test yesterday.   taked   took

2. There _____ frost on the ground.   was   were

3. Tommy _____ the Statue of Liberty.   seen   saw

4. Claire _____ her lizard to school.   brought   brang

5. Have you _____ my dog?   seen   saw

6. Alyssa _____ a new pair of skates.   gots   has

7. You _____ supposed to finish your work.   are   is

8. We _____ standing near a snake!   were   was

9. They _____ a pig in the mud.   seen   saw

10. We _____ our winter boots.   wore   weared

11. _____ your cat climb trees?   Do   Does

12. Rosie _____ cookies to the bake sale.   brang   brought

© Scholastic Inc.

An Apple a Day

Find the word that is incorrect in each sentence.
Cross it out and write the correct word on the line

1. Laura brang a snack to camp. _____

2. I seen sea lions at the beach. _____

3. Drew gots a dinosaur collection. _____

4. Mara taked her dog for a walk. _____

5. We is going to see the movie. _____

6. Jason runned to the playground. _____

7. How many pennies do you got? _____

8. The kids was having fun. _____

9. Did you saw the soccer game? _____

10. How much do that cost? _____

11. Kelly brang her cat to school! _____

12. I does my homework after school. _____

© Scholastic Inc.

Tales of Nature

Finish the stories by writing a sentence about each of the last two pictures.

Sentences should be written in the correct order to tell a story.

First: Two birds build a nest.

Next: _____

Last: _____

First: A flower bud grows.

Next: _____

Last: _____

© Scholastic Inc.

Stories on Parade

Stories have a beginning (B), a middle (M), and an end (E). Write a middle sentence that tells what happens next. Then write an ending sentence that tells what happens last.

(B) During the parade, a big balloon got loose in the wind.

(M) Next, _____

(E) Last, _____

(B) Five jugglers jumped out of a purple bus.

(M) Next, _____

(E) Last, _____

(B) A group of horses stopped right in front of us.

(M) Next, _____

(E) Last, _____

(B) Some veterans rode motorcycles.

(M) Next, _____

(E) Last, _____

© Scholastic Inc.

An Original Story

Choose a story idea from the list. Then write a beginning (B),
middle (M), and ending (E) sentence to make a story of your own.
Draw a picture to match each part.

The Best Birthday Ever   My Dog's Dream   The Magic Rock

B First: _____

_____

_____

_____

M Next: _____

_____

_____

_____

E Last: _____

_____

_____

_____

© Scholastic Inc.

Once Upon a Time

The **setting** of a story tells when or where it is happening.

Imagine that you are writing a story for each picture below. How will you describe the setting? Write a sentence describing each setting.

setting → characters → problem → solution

It was a hot morning in the desert.

All Kinds of Characters

Some characters are likable, and others are not.
Write a describing sentence about each character.
Be sure to give each character a name.

> The people or animals in a story are called characters.

setting → characters → problem → solution

_____

_____

_____

_____

_____

_____

_____

_____

© Scholastic Inc.

That's a Problem!

Think about each character in the sentences below. What could happen that would make a problem for that character? Write the next sentence creating a problem.

To make a story exciting, one of the characters often runs into a **problem**.

setting → characters → problem → solution

1 Beauty Butterfly was enjoying the warm spring day.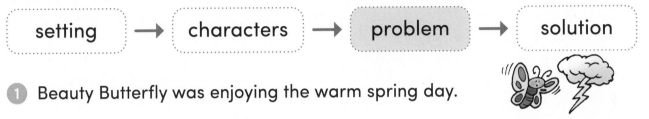

_____

2 Jesse was supposed to wear shoes outside.

_____

3 Gabriel could not wait to bite into his apple.

_____

4 Ben smacked the baseball into the air.

_____

5 Barney Bass had never seen such a big worm!

_____

© Scholastic Inc.

Map a story: Solution

Good Solution!

Read the beginning and middle parts of the stories below. Write an ending solution for each.

> At the end of the story, the problem is usually solved. This is called the **solution**.

setting → characters → problem → solution

David and his dog, Spot, were best friends. They went everywhere together. At bedtime, David whistled for Spot to jump in his bed. One winter night, David whistled and whistled, but Spot did not come.

_____

_____

_____

Josh loved second grade, but he did not like recess. Josh's class was always the last one out to the playground. Every day, Josh ran to get a swing, but they were always taken.

_____

_____

_____

© Scholastic Inc.

The Mighty Knight

A **story map** helps you plan the setting, characters, problem, and solution.

Write a sentence about each part of the map to make a story.

_____

_____

_____

_____

_____

_____

_____

A Story Fit for a King

Complete the map.
Then use it to write a story "fit for a king."

Use a story map to help plan your story before you begin writing.

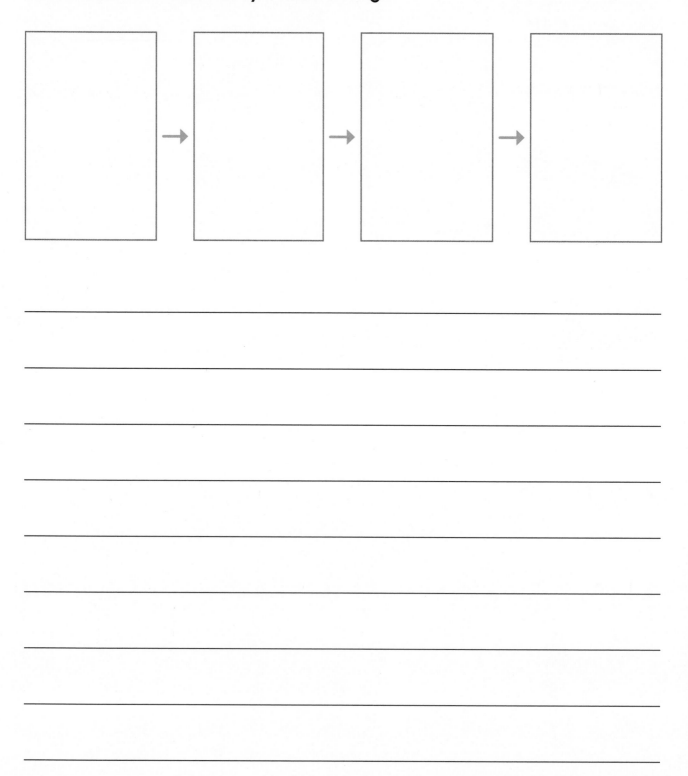

© Scholastic Inc.

Camp Friends

Use the proofreading marks to correct 10 mistakes in the letter.

mars⎹ = Make a capital letter.	? = Add a question mark.	! = Add an exclamation point.
⊙ = Add a period.	, = Add a comma.	☐∧ = Add a word. (Write a describing word in the box.)

October 15, 2020

Dear Friend,

the last time we saw each other, we were

at Camp Forest It was such a fun summer

Since then, I have spent my summers

traveling with my family We visited Italy

spain, and france last year The year

before that, we spent our whole summer

visiting different national parks in the

United States. it was an amazing trip!

What have your summers been like!

Sincerely,

David Alemano

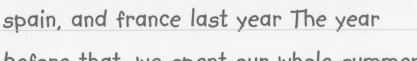
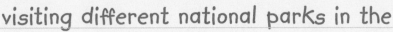

© Scholastic Inc.

Pen Pals

Use the five parts to write a letter to a friend about how you spend your summers. Be sure to proofread your letter for mistakes.

A **friendly letter** has five parts: date, greeting, body, closing, and signature.

_____
(today's date)

_____
(greeting)

_____

(body)

_____

_____

_____

_____

_____

_____

_____
(closing)

_____
(your name)

© Scholastic Inc.

ANSWER KEY

Page 5
Many of, Our teacher, The reading, The globe, We study, Our class

Page 6
1. The blue whale has no teeth.
2. The blue whale is the largest animal in the world.
3. Blue whales are not part of the fish family.
4. Blue whales eat tiny shrimp-like sea creatures.
5. Blue whales have two blowholes.

Page 7
Sentences will vary.

Page 8
1. Where is the king's castle?
2. Who helped Humpty Dumpty?
3. Why did the cow jump over the moon?
4. Will the frog become a prince?
5. Could the three mice see?

Page 9
Sentences will vary.

Page 10
1. The sun is the closest star to Earth.
2. The sun is not the brightest star.
3. What is the temperature of the sun?
4. The sun is a ball of hot gas.
5. How large is the sun?
6. It takes about eight minutes for the sun's light to reach Earth.

Page 11
Sentences will vary.

Page 12
1. capital letter 2. period
3. question mark

Dear Mom and Dad,

Camp is so cool? today we went swimming? do you know what I like best about camp. fishing is my favorite thing to do. did you feed my hamster. I really miss you?

Love,
Dalton

Sentences will vary.

Page 13
1. . 2. ? 3. ! 4. ? 5. . 6. ! 7. ?
8. . 9. ? 10. ! 11. . 12. ?

Page 14
Sentences will vary.

Page 15
Lists will vary.

Page 16
Lists and sentences will vary.

Page 17
Sample answers:
2. A cat plays with fish in the living room.
3. A bunny eats a carrot in the garden.

Page 18
Sentences and pictures will vary.

Page 19
Answers will vary. Possible answers:
1. fat, three 2. wooden, warm
3. Orange, sunny 4. lazy, muddy
5. thirsty, shallow 6. funny, black

Page 20
1. fluffy 2. hard 3. fuzzy
4. sharp 5. soft

```
S  C (R  O  U  G  H) G (T) H
H  S  Y  K  V  A  D  M  H  E
I  Q (B  U  M  P  Y) X  I  L
N (S  M  O  O  T  H) O  C  H
Y  U  T  R (S  T  I  C  K  Y)
```

Page 21
Lists of words will vary.

Page 22
Describing words will vary.

Page 23
Sentences will vary.

Page 24
Sentences will vary.

Page 25
Sentences will vary.

Page 26
2. We blew up orange and green balloons.
3. We ate cake and ice cream.
4. The cake frosting was blue and yellow.
5. We made a bookmark and a clay pot.
6. We brought games and presents.

Page 27
2. The first graders and second graders eat lunch at noon.
3. The napkins and forks are on the table.
4. Are the muffins and cookies in the oven?
5. Michael and Stephen brought lunch today.

Page 28
1. Fill a cup with water and add some flower seeds.
2. This will soften the seeds because they are hard.
3. Fill another cup with dirt while the seeds soak in water.
4. Bury the seeds in the cup until the dirt covers them.
5. Add water to the plant but do not add too much.
6. Set the cup in the sun so the plant will grow.

Page 29
Sentences will vary.

Page 30
Sentences will vary.

Page 31
Sentences will vary.

Page 32
Check that children have used the appropriate proofreading marks to fix the sentences. Describing words will vary.
1. Sometimes I can see Mars, Jupiter, and Saturn with my telescope.
2. There are many stars in our galaxy.
3. Comets are large pieces of ice and rock.
4. The sun is really a huge star.
5. Is there life on any other planet?
6. Look at that beautiful shooting star!
7. Can you imagine traveling in space?

Page 33
Describing words will vary. Saturn is famous for the rings that surround it. Its rings are made of ice, rock, and dirt. The rings circle around the planet. Saturn is made mostly of gas. Saturn's gases are lighter than water. That means Saturn would float if you put it into a tub of water. Saturn has more than 60 moons.

Page 34
1. took **2.** was **3.** saw
4. brought **5.** seen **6.** has
7. are **8.** were **9.** saw
10. wore **11.** Does **12.** brought

Page 35
1. ~~brang~~, brought
2. ~~seen~~, saw
3. ~~gots~~, has
4. ~~taked~~, took
5. ~~is~~, are
6. ~~runned~~, ran
7. ~~got~~, have
8. ~~was~~, were
9. ~~saw~~, see
10. ~~do~~, does
11. ~~brang~~, brought
12. ~~does~~, do

Page 36
Sentences will vary.

Page 37
Sentences will vary.

Page 38
Stories will vary.

Page 39
Sentences will vary.

Page 40
Sentences will vary.

Page 41
Sentences will vary.

Page 42
Answers will vary.

Page 43
Stories will vary.

Page 44
Stories will vary.

Page 45
October 15, 2020
Dear Friend,
the last time we saw each other, we were at Camp Forest. It was such a fun summer. Since then, I have spent my summers traveling with my family. We visited Italy, spain, and france last year. The year before that, we spent our whole summer visiting different national parks in the United States. it was an amazing trip! What have your summers been like?
Sincerely,
David Alemano

Page 46
Letters will vary.

© Scholastic Inc.